The Colour Violet

m. r. wolfe

Presentation by *BookLeaf Publishing*

Web: www.bookleafpub.com

E-mail: info@bookleafpub.com

ISBN:9789358317879

First edition 2023

DEDICATION

To my younger self who had no voice

ACKNOWLEDGEMENT

Thank you to my dear friend Steph who
encouraged me to write and publish these poems

PREFACE

To all my readers, I want to be as raw and honest as I can be however I don't have a comfortable environment to do so, therefore I've created a pen name that will allow me to be closer to you than I am to the people who know me in real life.

Pink Swords

Choked up
Stuck in my throat
A mix of salmon pink liquid swords
Stuck in my throat
My mind has become too great a well
And I'm running out of water
Because I keep taking buckets out of it,
The more water I take out,
The more stars disappear from the sky
The more I realised there weren't
Any stars to begin with
choked up,
I'm stuck in my throat

How Much Does It Cost?

My body is not a temple
It's never felt that way
It's why I'm treated the way I am
It's why people feel the need to tack
on my value
It's heavy
and It's weighing me down
Pale cream roots cover my worst parts
And hold me in place
Like I'm strapped to a chair
On a ride I can't get off
A ride I never asked for
In seats that weren't built for me
Who were these seats built for?

Just One More

Just one more almost fate
Just one more drink
Just one more tear soaked pillow

Just one more try
Just one more sun rise
Just one more night of wishing I could join the
stars
Just one more bite
Just one more time my mother would say
You should exercise more
Just one more first date
Just one more rejection

Just one more day of fearing death
Just one more day of fearing a long life

Just one more time
and it'll all be worth it

Almost Held Together

Now my tears are black
My confidence has bled out
From all the tiny scars by love I lack
with too much darkness comes fallout

No one minds if you're the only one that gets
hurt
Not even me.
Nothing looks wrong until it's overt
It's fine to let me be

The War in my Head

Don't   Eat It.
Don't   Eat It.
Don't   Eat It.
Don't   Eat It.
Don't   Eat It.
Don't   Eat It.
Don't   Eat It.

Voices in my Head

The voices in my head
(why does she sound like my mother?)
Tell me everyone hates me?
They'd rather see me if I were dead
I know what I lack is clarity
But how am I meant to see,
If my tears are black?

Three Meals A Day

They tell me to eat this bowl of razors and
expect flowers to grow in my stomach.
I swallow each one down as if addicted to the
pain.
I keep going,
no matter how much my mind screams
Stop.
Stop.
Stop.
Please.

The Little Voice

Sometimes the things you say make me feel
small
And so sometimes I wish that I could be so
small that I just disappear altogether
Because maybe then
I could just exist

Intimacy

Why are the intimacies of sex not intimate at all?
Your fingers glide over every bump, on every
stretch of skin.
I'm naked, but not really
Naked like the empty shelves and cupboards left
behind when you move
out of a place you've always known
We're so close yet I cannot feel you
Who are you?
I don't recognise my reflection
Why are intimates of sex not intimate at all?

Last Place

My crush turns into obsession
And obsession into depression
I guess that's what fuels creative expression
But I'm tired of learning lessons
I'm tired of feeling less than
It's a place I put myself in

To Someone Who Doesn't Deserve It

In this moment I thought I was in love with you
Muffled music coloured the room blue
Nothing but just us two
To stop myself from drowning in your eyes
I stared up at the starry night skies
You washed over me like waves
The words we exchanged covered us like
blankets to keep us warm
In this moment I thought I was in love with you

If only you loved me too.

Gravity Is Against Me

Why do you draw me in
Like Elara to Jupiter
When a natural disaster will
Undoubtedly make itself known
I don't reach for a rose and
Hope it pricks me
The mistake we all seem to make
Is the assumption that traveling on the ocean
will lead to some safe harbour

What if there is no harbour?

Curly Hair

I get caught in the knots of my curly hair
Especially when I'm told it should be straight
It'd be better if it were straight
It would be easier if it were straight
But I don't think that's who I am
Maybe I was meant to have knots in my hair
Curls that tangle in ever part of my life
Knots can be beauty too

One Of My Rock Bottoms

I was close to it once
It was painless
Life dulled down to comforting quiet
The Christmas lights glittering in the reflection
of my mirror

I wanted to be one of those lights
A hand hung limp at the edge of my bed

But reality rushed back
In black puddles all over the floor

The Grave of Flowers

I can't tell if the beauty of life is meant to
distract or save you
White clouds drifting in the gentle sky
like the ones little kids drew
Or the thousands of crystals that decorate
it at night like jewelry

Just out of reach
Like a comforting memory

You look behind you
At a small buried plot of land
Flowers that should be beautiful
stuffed in the ground like a headstone

Self-inflicted Pain

There's a tightness in my chest
A sinking feeling
An overwhelming pain that won't let me rest
Over tiny little things, I shouldn't be left reeling
I panic for a bit
And let the illogical take over
Who put this knife in my stomach?

I've Never Felt So Distant

Who are these strangers in my house
Pretending to be my family
You're not my mother
You're not my sister
Who are these strangers in my house
Dressing in my sisters clothes
Putting on my mother's robes
Who are these strangers in my house
I ask my dad, but he thinks I'm crazy
He can't see these people
Are wearing my mother's skin
And my stealing my sister's height
Who let them in?

Enjoy the Ride

You made me want to be better
Try harder, be better
But so quickly did you throw me away
So quickly did you give up on me
I guess I do it too
I give up on me over and over
And over
And over
And over
I wanted to be better
But I'm strapped into a ride on a roller coaster
That's not built for me
They yell at you and say that seat is for you.
You must sit there
And you will enjoy the ride
If you don't sit there and enjoy you're doing
something wrong

But this seat wasn't built for me
I don't fit
So how can you say its for me
How can you say I should enjoy it
When I never wanted to go on the fucking ride
in the first place

A Love Letter

Hurt people, hurt people
But sometimes they help
They see someone who's hurt the same way they
were
and become the person for them that no one was
before
A hand reaches down to pick up the pieces
Scattered on the floor
And when I put it together I realised it was my
reflection in the mirror that I was trying to save

To: The Reader

How do you help someone feel less alone than
you felt
When you feel so inadequate
Words teeter out the gaps of your lips
with the intent of understanding
But they fall short
They're slobbering all over the sides
like the messiest cheeseburger
with hope that you still like how it tastes
I think it tastes alright
because I'm finally starting to feel less hungry.
And that's all we can hope for.

From:

I just want to let you know,
I'm here with you
When every nerve in your body is singed
Please know I've been through it too

I've been swimming through liquid worlds
So I know it's hard to breathe too.

Don't let them make you feel small
because even the tiniest of voices matter.

I've been where you are
Sometimes I still am
But I'm still here
And so are you.
You
Are
Here.

I promise you it's temporary
Just wait a little longer
Distract yourself a little longer
And I'll be waiting here
In these words
For you.

from: a dream I once had
to: